Explorando el espacio con una astronauta

Exploring Space with an Astronaut

Patricia J. Murphy

Enslow Elementary

an imprint of

Enslow Publishers, Inc.

40 Industrial Road
Box 398
Berkeley Heights, NJ 07922
USA

http://www.enslow.com

Contents

Contenido

Words to Know / Palabras a conocer

astronaut (AS troh nawt)—A person who goes into space.

black hole—A place in space with very strong gravity. Black holes can even pull in light and hold it down.

experiment (ek SPER ih ment)—A test done by scientists.

gravity (GRAV ih tee)—A force that pulls things toward larger things. Earth's gravity keeps people and other things on the ground.

space shuttle (SPAYSS SHUHT uhl)—A spacecraft used to take astronauts to space and back to Earth.

telescope (TEL e skohp)—A tool that makes objects look larger.

universe (YOO nih vurss)—Everything in space. The universe is the stars, planets, and everything else.

astronauta—Persona que va al espacio.

agujero negro—Lugar en el espacio donde la gravedad es muy fuerte. Los agujeros negros pueden hasta jalar luz a su interior y evitar que salga.

experimento—Prueba que hacen los científicos.

gravedad—Fuerza que jala las cosas hacia otras cosas más grandes. La gravedad de la Tierra mantiene a las personas y otros objetos sobre el suelo.

transbordador espacial—Aeronave que se usa para llevar a los astronautas al espacio y de regreso a la Tierra.

telescopio—Herramienta que hace que los objetos se vean más grandes.

universo—Todo lo que hay en el espacio. El universo incluye las estrellas, los planetas y todo lo demás.

3 . . . 2 . . . 1 . . . Lift-off!

A space shuttle climbs high
into the sky. Inside the shuttle,
astronauts are on their way to
learn more about space.

¡Despegamos!

3 . . . 2 . . . 1 . . .
¡Despegamos!

Un transbordador espacial
se eleva por el cielo. A bordo
del transbordador los
astronautas van en camino
a aprender más sobre el
espacio.

An astronaut is a person who goes into space. Astronauts fly on a space shuttle.

¿Qué hace un astronauta?

Un astronauta es una persona que viaja al espacio. Los astronautas viajan en un transbordador espacial.

4

The space shuttle takes off like a rocket.
It lands like an airplane.

El transbordador espacial despega como
los cohetes. Aterriza como los aviones.

Meet Eileen Collins.

Eileen Collins is an astronaut. She was the first woman to be a space shuttle pilot. She was also the first woman to be the leader of a space shuttle trip.

Ella es Eileen Collins.

Eileen Collins es astronauta. Fue la primera mujer que se convirtió en piloto del transbordador espacial. Además fue la primera mujer en dirigir un viaje en un transbordador espacial.

6

She and four other astronauts worked as a team. Some astronauts flew the space shuttle. Others did experiments.

Ella y otros cuatro astronautas trabajaron como equipo. Algunos astronautas conducían el transbordador espacial. Otros hacían experimentos.

How do astronauts live in space?

In the space shuttle, astronauts float everywhere. Sleeping bags are tied to walls. Toilets have a type of seat belt.

¿Cómo viven los astronautas en el espacio?

En el transbordador espacial, los astronautas flotan por todos lados. Las bolsas para dormir están amarradas a las paredes. Los inodoros tienen un cinturón de seguridad.

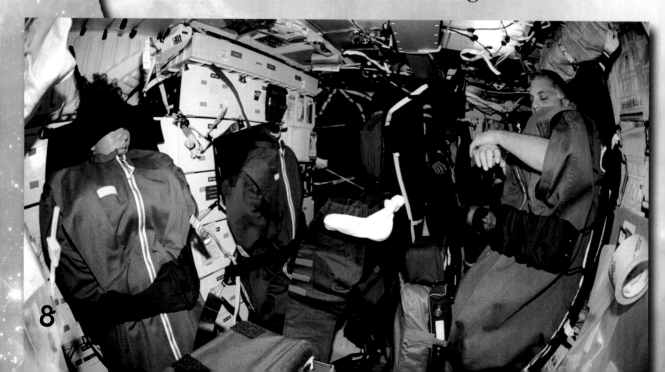

Astronauts exercise to stay strong.
They take sponge baths to keep clean.

Los astronautas
hacen ejercicio para
mantenerse fuertes.
Se dan baños con
esponja para
mantenerse limpios.

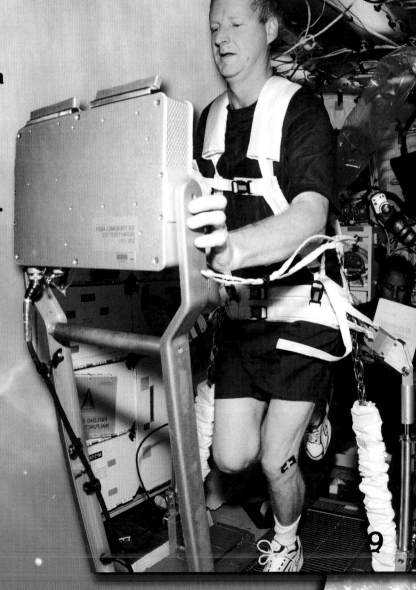

Why do astronauts go into space? *****

Astronauts test ways to live and work in a world that is very different from Earth. In space, there is no up and down, no air, and the Sun always shines.

¿Por qué los astronautas van al espacio?

Los astronautas prueban maneras de vivir y trabajar en un mundo muy diferente a la Tierra. En el espacio no hay arriba ni abajo, no hay aire y siempre hay Sol.

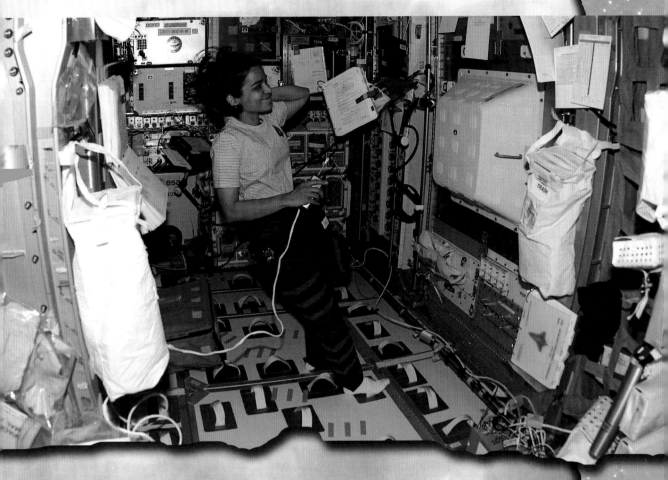

Astronauts do experiments. They look for problems and fix them. This will make space travel safer.

Los astronautas hacen experimentos. Buscan problemas y los solucionan. Esto hará que el viaje por el espacio sea más seguro.

11

What tools do astronauts use?

A space shuttle is a giant toolbox! It holds tools, like computers that help fly the space shuttle.

¿Qué herramientas usan los astronautas?

Un transbordador espacial es una gigantesca caja de herramientas. Lleva herramientas, como computadoras que ayudan a conducir el transbordador espacial.

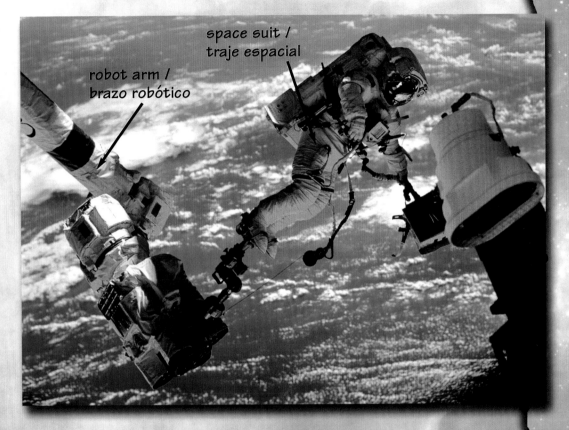

space suit /
traje espacial

robot arm /
brazo robótico

Astronauts use robot arms to move things and
people outside the shuttle. On space walks, space
suits keep astronauts safe.

Los astronautas usan brazos robóticos para mover
cosas y personas fuera del transbordador. Cuando
los astronautas salen a dar caminatas espaciales,
sus trajes los protegen.

13

The crew's special job ✳✳✳✳✳✳✳✳✳✳✳✳✳

Eileen Collins and her crew had a special job to do. They took an X-ray telescope into space with them.

El trabajo especial de la tripulación

Eileen Collins y su tripulación tenían un trabajo especial. Llevaron un telescopio de rayos X al espacio.

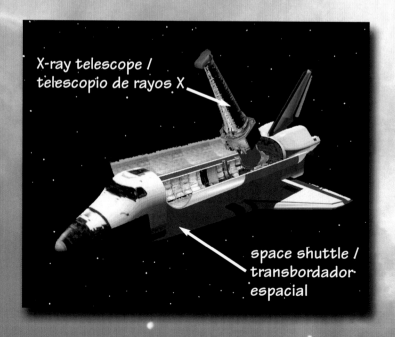

X-ray telescope /
telescopio de rayos X

space shuttle /
transbordador
espacial

14

X-ray telescope, named *Chandra* /
telescopio de rayos X llamado Chandra

First, they tested the telescope. Next, they flipped some switches and let the telescope go into space. Then the telescope used its rockets to fly higher into space.

Primero, probaron el telescopio. Luego, movieron algunos interruptores y dejaron que el telescopio se fuera al espacio. Luego el telescopio usó sus cohetes para volar más alto en el espacio.

What does the X-ray telescope do? ✳✳✳✳

An X-ray telescope sees light that is too strong for our eyes. It sees gas and light being pulled into black holes.

a black hole /
agujero negro

¿Para qué sirve el telescopio de rayos X?

Un telescopio de rayos X ve luz que es demasiado fuerte para nuestros ojos. Ve gas y luz que entran en los agujeros negros.

The telescope sends important pictures back to Earth. These pictures show scientists new things in the **universe**.

El telescopio envía importantes imágenes a la Tierra. Estas imágenes les muestran a los científicos cosas nuevas que hay en el universo.

an exploding star /
explosión de una estrella

Do the astronauts do other jobs? ✳✳✳✳✳

Yes. They did experiments with plants and exercise machines. They were studying life without gravity.

¿Hacen otros trabajos los astronautas?

Sí. Hacen experimentos con plantas y con máquinas de ejercicio. Están estudiando la vida sin gravedad.

Plant experiment / Experimento con plantas

When there was some time to rest, the astronauts could look out their window. They saw Earth from many, many miles away!

Cuando tienen tiempo para descansar, los astronautas pueden asomarse por la ventana. ¡Ven la Tierra desde muchas millas de distancia!

Rocky Mountains in Colorado /
Montañas Rocallosas de Colorado

Would you like to fly into space?

Do you like math and science? Do you like to visit new places? Do you like fast roller coasters? Astronauts do, too! Maybe someday you will become an astronaut, just like Eileen Collins.

¿Te gustaría ir al espacio?

¿Te gustan las matemáticas y la ciencia? ¿Te gusta visitar nuevos lugares? ¿Te gustan las montañas rusas veloces? ¡A los astronautas también les gusta todo eso! Quizá algún día te conviertas en astronauta como Eileen Collins.

What is in your night sky?

You will need:

✔ journal ✔ pencil ✔ flashlight

1. Go outside at night with an adult. Look at the Moon and the stars. Draw what you see. Ask questions like: What is the shape of the moon? What stars look brightest? Write about the night sky in your journal.

2. Watch the sky every night for a month. Do this at the same time each night. How does the sky change? How does it stay the same? Write down what you think in your journal.

¿Qué hay en el cielo nocturno?

Necesitarás:

✔ diario ✔ lápiz ✔ linterna

1. Sal en la noche con un adulto. Mira la Luna y las estrellas. Dibuja lo que ves. Haz preguntas como: ¿Qué forma tiene la Luna? ¿Qué estrella brilla más? Escribe sobre el cielo nocturno en tu diario.

2. Observa el cielo cada noche durante un mes. Hazlo a la misma hora cada noche. ¿Cómo cambia el cielo? ¿Qué cosas no cambian? Escribe lo que piensas en tu diario.

**The changing view of the Moon /
La vista cambiante de la Luna**

Learn More / Más para aprender

Books / Libros

In English / En inglés

Bredeson, Carmen. *Astronauts*. New York: Children's Press, 2003.

Hayden, Kate. *Astronaut, Living in Space*. New York: Dorling Kindersley, 2000.

Shearer, Deborah A. *Astronauts at Work*. Mankato, Minn.: Capstone Press, Inc., 2002.

In Spanish / En español

Bredeson, Carmen. *Astronautas*. New York: Children's Press, 2004.

Bredeson, Carmen. *Nave espacial*. New York, Children's Press, 2004.

Internet Addresses / Direcciones de Internet

In English / En inglés

The Kennedy Space Center
<http://www.ksc.nasa.gov>

NASA Kids
<http://kids.msfc.nasa.gov>

In Spanish / En español

NASA Space Place
<http://spaceplace.jpl.nasa.gov/sp/kids/>

Index

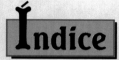

Índice

❧ *In memory of the space shuttle* Columbia *crew* ❧

Note to Teachers and Parents: The *I Like Science!* series supports the National Science Education Standards for K–4 science, including content standards "Science as a human endeavor" and "Science as inquiry." The Words to Know section introduces subject-specific vocabulary, including pronunciation and definitions. Early readers may require help with these new words.

Enslow Elementary, an imprint of Enslow Publishers, Inc.
Enslow Elementary® is a registered trademark of Enslow Publishers, Inc.

Bilingual edition copyright 2008 by Enslow Publishers, Inc. Originally published in English under the title *Exploring Space with an Astronaut* © 2004 by Enslow Publishers, Inc. Bilingual edition translated by Nora Diaz, edited by María Cristina Mella, of Strictly Spanish, LLC.

All rights reserved.

No part of this book may be reproduced by any means without the written permission of the publisher.

Library of Congress Cataloging-in-Publication Data

Murphy, Patricia J., 1963–
[Exploring space with an astronaut. Spanish & English]
Explorando el espacio con una astronauta = Exploring space with an astronaut / Patricia J. Murphy.
p. cm. — (I like science! Bilingual)
Summary: "Discusses astronauts and space exploration"—Provided by publisher.
Includes bibliographical references and index.
ISBN-13: 978-0-7660-2977-4
ISBN-10: 0-7660-2977-8
1. Astronautics—Juvenile literature. 2. Outer space—Exploration—Juvenile literature. 3. Astronauts—Juvenile literature.
I. Title.
TL793.M83718 2004
629.4—dc22
2007011588

Printed in the United States of America

122011 The HF Group, North Manchester, IN

10 9 8 7 6 5 4 3 2

To Our Readers: We have done our best to make sure all Internet Addresses in this book were active and appropriate when we went to press. However, the author and the publisher have no control over and assume no liability for the material available on those Internet sites or on other Web sites they may link to. Any comments or suggestions can be sent by e-mail to comments@enslow.com or to the address on the back cover.

Photo Credits: All photos courtesy of National Aeronautics and Space Administration (NASA), except p. 21 (U.S. Naval Observatory).

Cover Photo: NASA

Series Literacy Consultant:
Allan A. De Fina, Ph.D.
Past President of the New Jersey Reading Association
Professor, Department of Literacy Education
New Jersey City University

Science Consultant:
Marianne J. Dyson
Former NASA Flight Controller